I0482979

THE ELEVEN BY FIFTEEN EXPLORATIONS

Laura Kitching

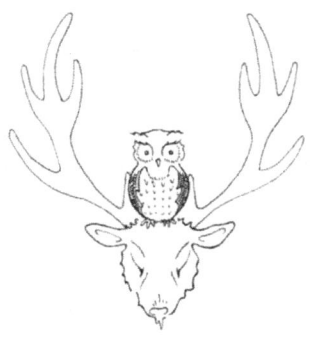

— Elk & Owl Books—

ISBN-13: 978-1496034755
ISBN-10: 1496034759

www.elkandowl.com

The Eleven by Fifteen Explorations

One:

Sometimes the mountains went missing.

Two:

They were too far away to determine whether the lifeforms were gargantuan, or the terrain rather small.

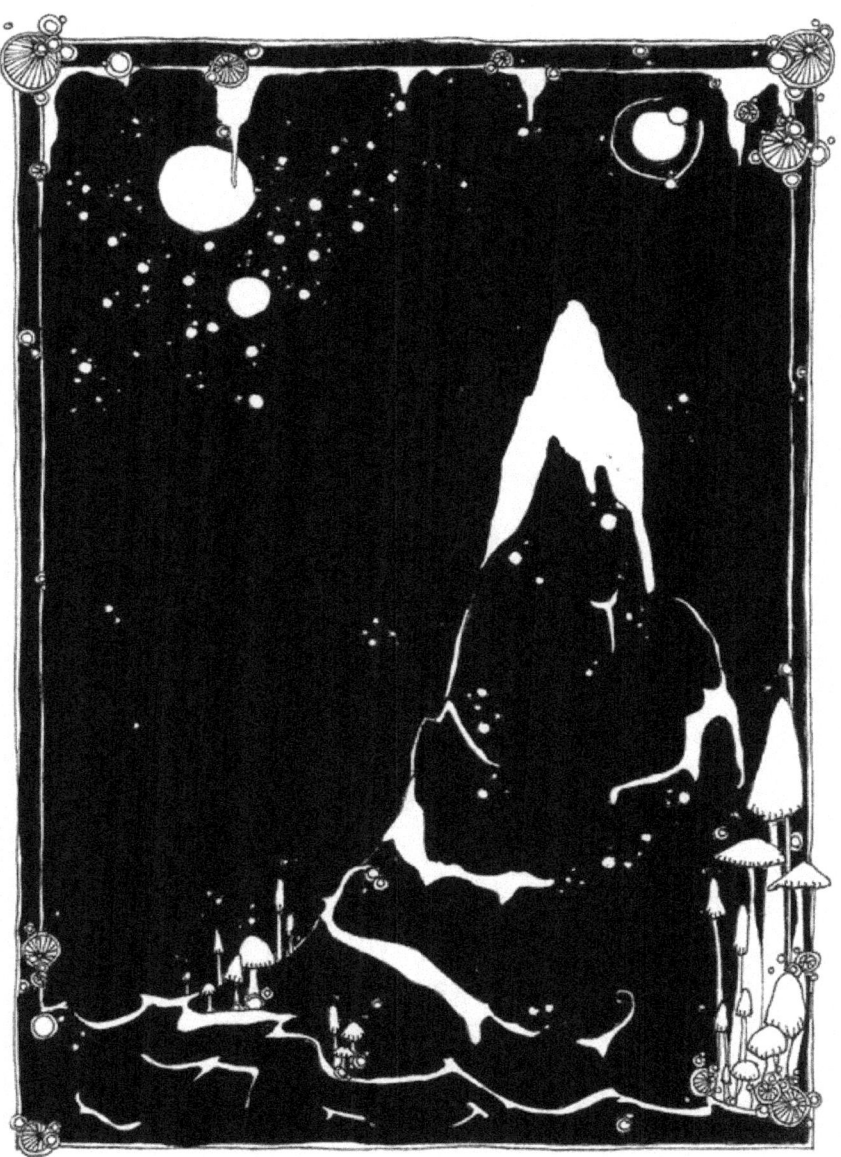

Three:

The repositioning of geological structures.

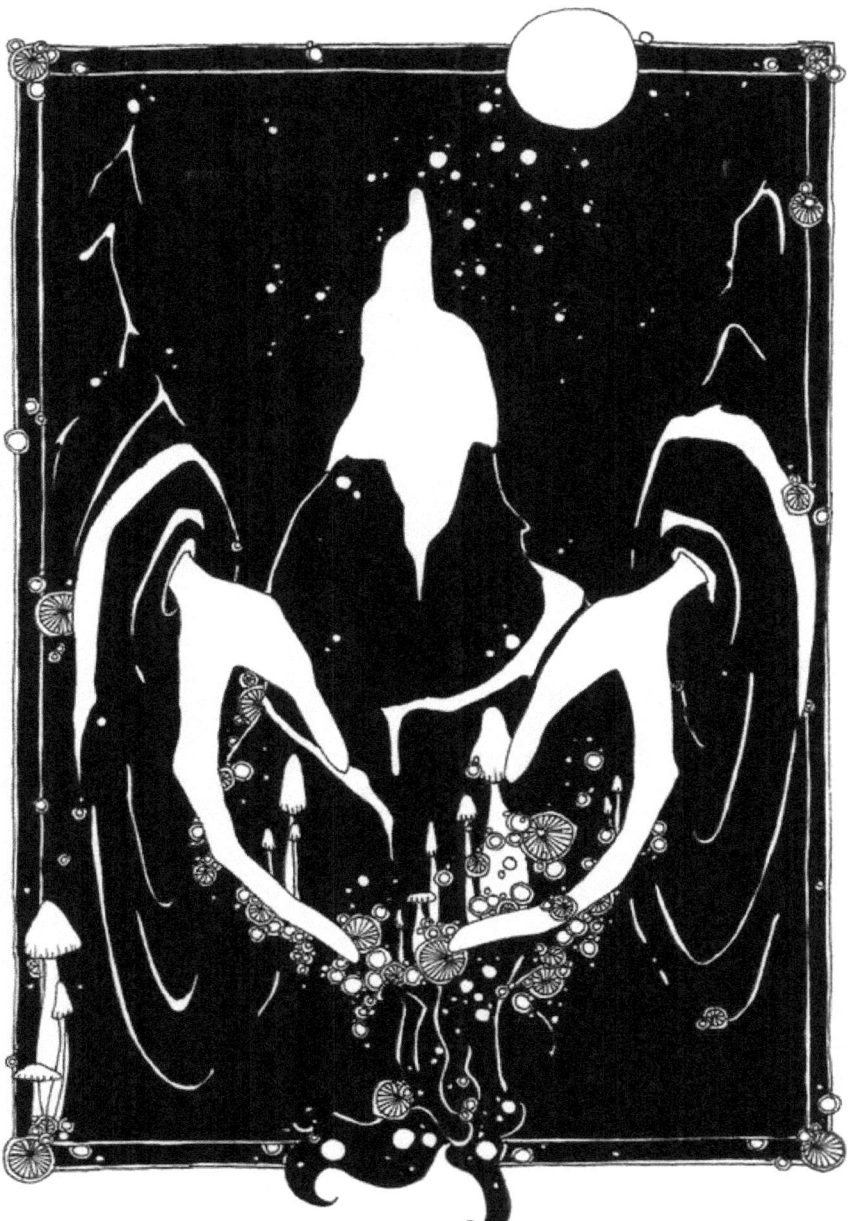

Four:

The holes solidified into Mountains.

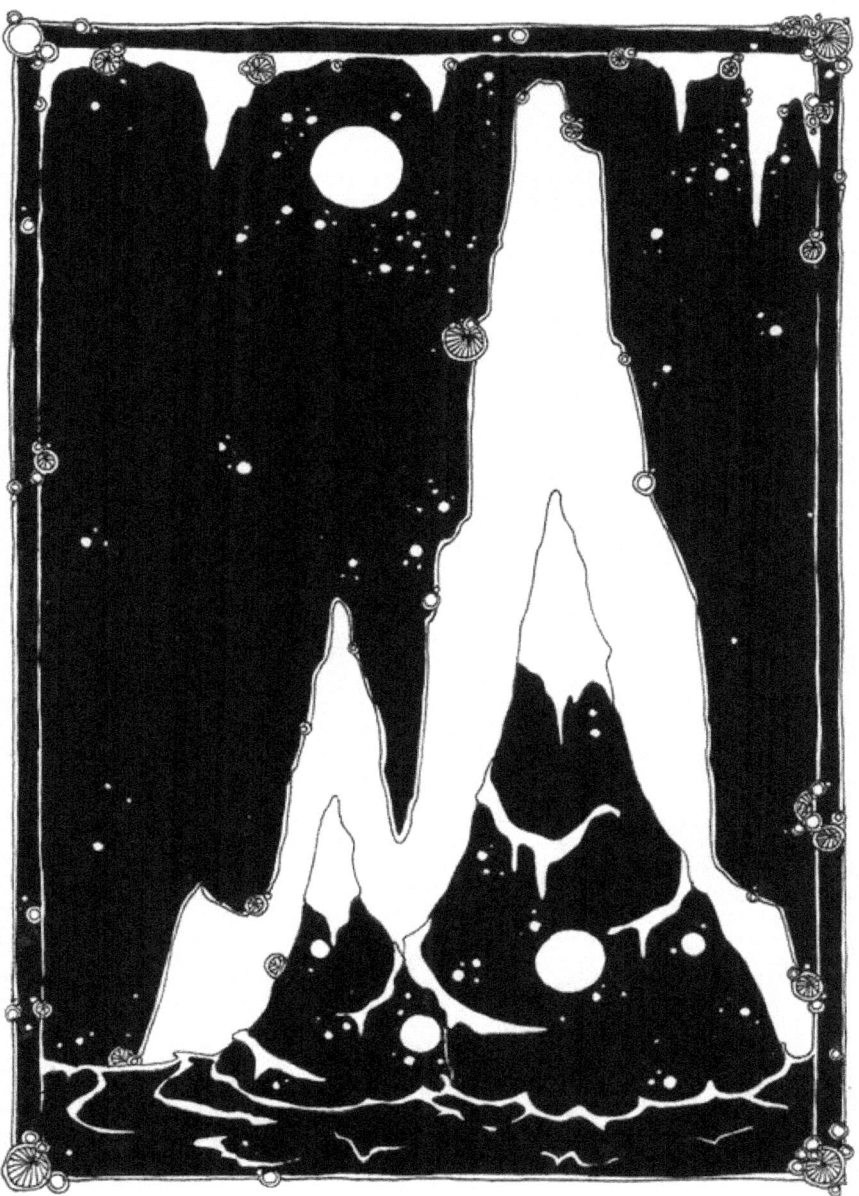

Five:

Methods of replanting.

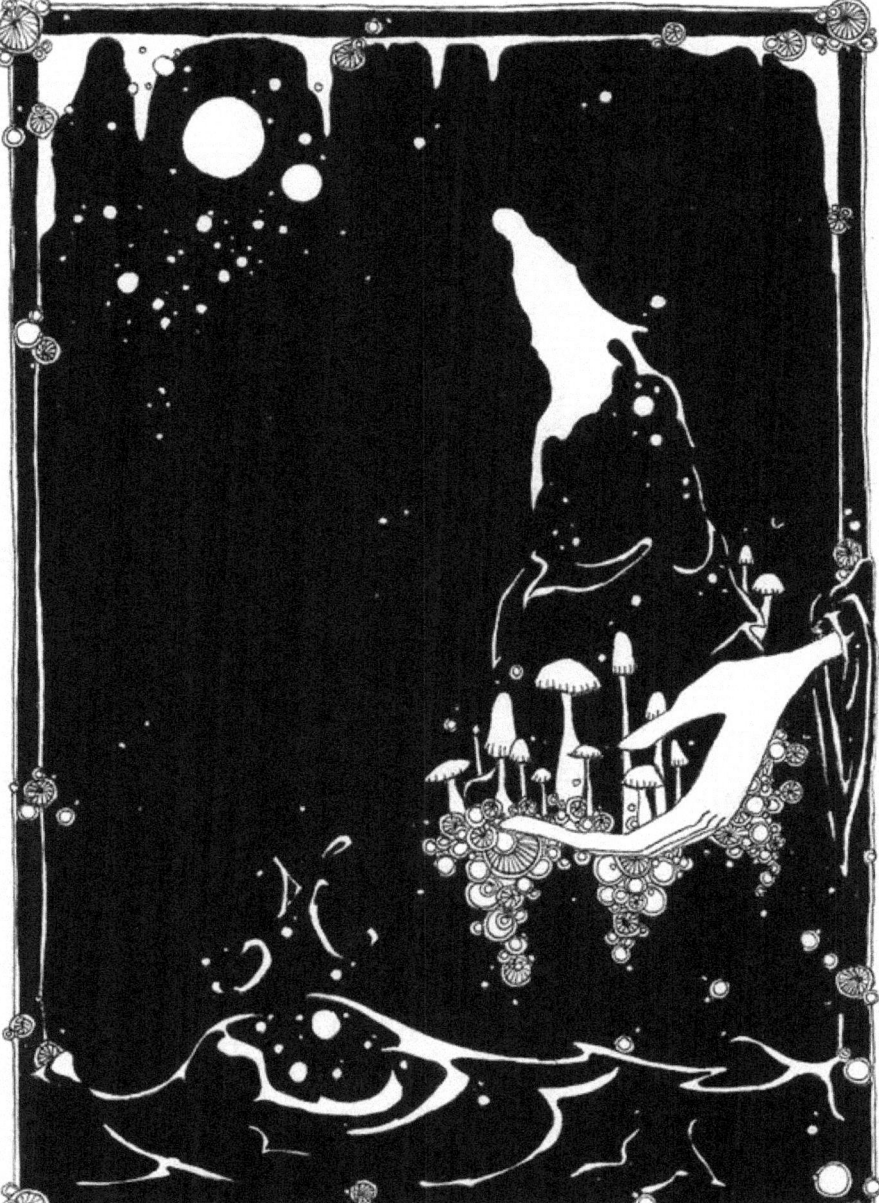

Six:

The lunarescent sea.

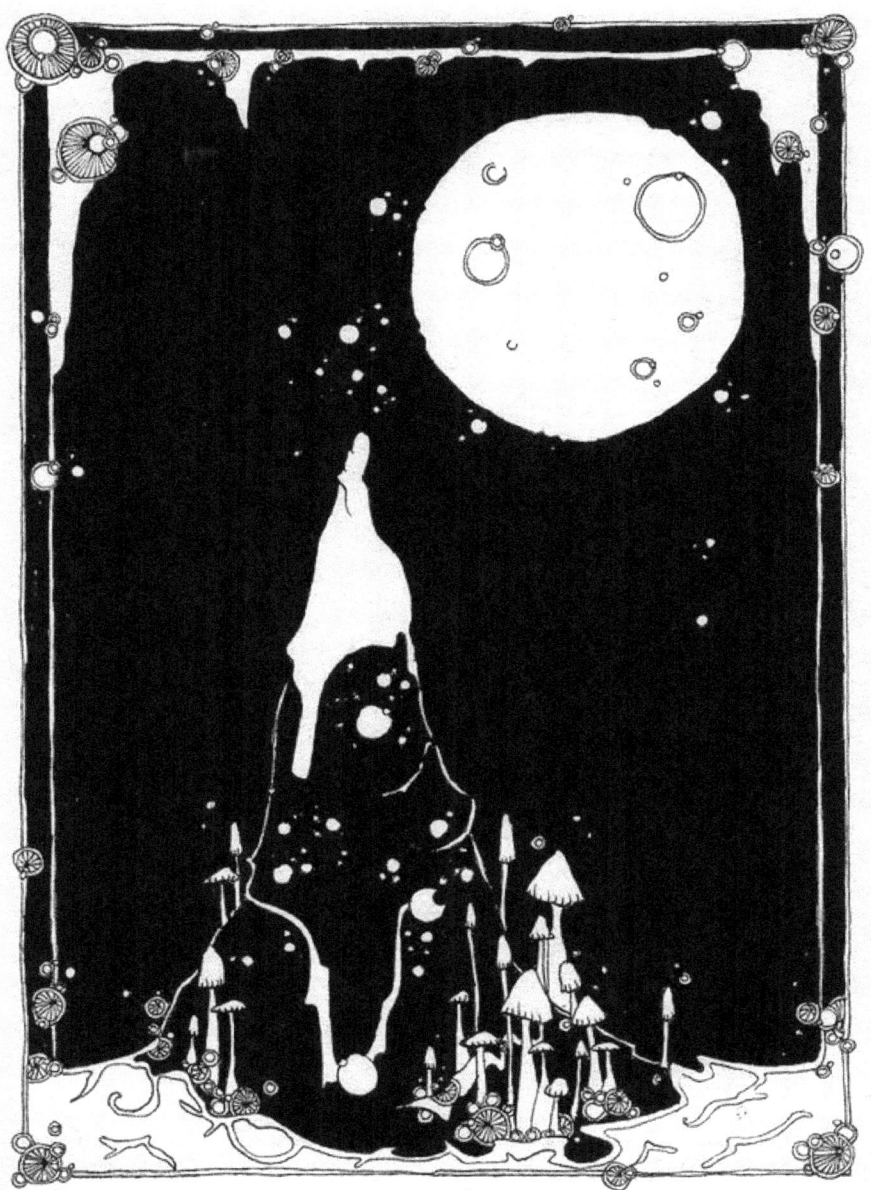

ABOUT LAURA

Laura Kitching was born in Scotland and studied fine art and writing in Devon, where she discovered a liking for hiding things, old science books, and fungus. She's slightly obsessed with drawing circles, and dreams of one day owning a sofa.

She thinks rabbits are a little bit sinister.

To find more of Laura's work, visit: elkandowl.com

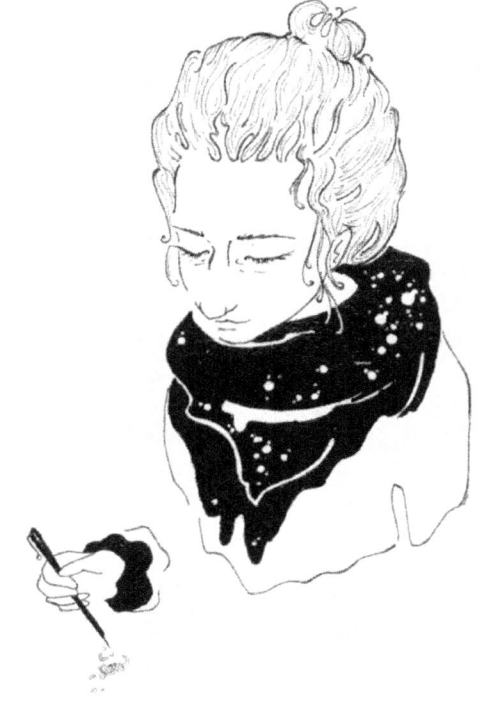